The
Young Person's
Guide to
Self-Coaching

S U

7 STEPS TO SUCCEED!

C
E
E
D

PAM RICHARDSON

AuthorHouse™ UK
1663 Liberty Drive
Bloomington, IN 47403 USA
www.authorhouse.co.uk
UK TFN: 0800 0148641 (Toll Free inside the UK)
UK Local: 02036 956322 (+44 20 3695 6322 from outside the UK)

Because of the dynamic nature of the Internet, any web addresses or links contained in this book may have changed since publication and may no longer be valid. The views expressed in this work are solely those of the author and do not necessarily reflect the views of the publisher, and the publisher hereby disclaims any responsibility for them.

Any people depicted in stock imagery provided by Getty Images are models, and such images are being used for illustrative purposes only.
Certain stock imagery © Getty Images.

This book is printed on acid-free paper.

ISBN: 978-1-6655-8777-8 (sc)
ISBN: 978-1-6655-8778-5 (e)

Print information available on the last page.

Published by AuthorHouse 05/20/2021

authorHOUSE®

Coach yourself to SUCCEED!

Who is the expert of your life?   **You are!**

Find out more about yourself so that you SUCCEED in whatever you choose to do in your life. Here's how:

Sort out your values.

Understand yourself and others.

Change what you want to change.

Choose SMART goals.

Enjoy GROWing with your inner coach.

Energise your mind and body.

Design your *own* life.

Sort Out Your Values

Answer the following questions and you will start to see what makes you tick. Values are who you are! When you know what matters to you and you respect that, then you feel good about yourself and get on with other people.

Reflect:

When someone does something that goes against one of your values, it can make you feel angry, frustrated, or sad. Understanding this can help you to deal with this rather than just reacting and kicking off! You may have come up with words like *loyalty, trust, being there,* and *respect.*

Do: Fill the Post-it Notes with one word that describes what matters to *you* most.

These words describe who you truly are. Just for a moment, if you had to choose just one, which one would you hold onto?

How are you living in a way that shows this matters to you? Here's an example: 'We are all different, and I respect the differences.'

Understand Yourself

Reflect:

What do you believe about yourself?

Have you ever stopped to listen to what you are saying to yourself?

Do: Spend a few minutes listening to the chatter in your head. What do you hear? Write it down if you want to.

The next question is an obvious one! *How does it help you to hear yourself talk like this?* Clearly, it doesn't help.

Here are a few examples that young people have heard: 'Nobody likes me.' 'I always mess up.' 'I'm hopeless.' 'I don't know.' These are called 'limiting beliefs' or 'negative self-talk.'

So what would you choose to hear that is more supportive of yourself? Notice the word *choose*. You are in control of your brain! It needs to be trained to be positive and supportive of you. Not to repeat messages you may have heard in the past that you keep repeating now!

Nobody likes me.

I like me.

I always mess up.

It's OK to make mistakes.

I'm hopeless. I don't know.

I can do this. It's OK to ask.

Do: If you wrote anything down above, what would your helpful champion be saying now?

Make friends with your inner coach.
Who is this? It is the voice that

✓ is positive
✓ doesn't judge you
✓ believes in you
✓ encourages and supports you
✓ wants the best for you
✓ is unconditional
✓ is your best friend

Do:

1. **Listening only to the positive voice in your head takes practice. Keep practising!**

2. **When you hear anything negative, remember to remain as non-judgemental of yourself as you can. Be your own best friend.**

Understand Others

Who else are you?

You are three people. You thought you were only one!

For us to really understand ourselves, understand why we do what we do in different situations, we need to get to know all three.

So here goes. Let me introduce you to your PAC.

The three people inside you and me are called parent, adult, and child.

Parent tells us what to do and how and when to do it.

When we are very young, we learn by copying behaviour from people around us: parents, carers, grandparents, teachers, etc.

What kind of behaviour can we learn?

loving, caring, kind, helpful	bossy
non-judgemental	critical
encouraging	finding fault
supporting	controls behaviour
protects	power based
teaches	sets limits
gives advice	uses sanctions

Yes, we learn all of this and then copy from a very young age!

Adult is the wise part of us, which thinks things through and knows how to make decisions.

stores information
stays objective—decides what is and not what should be!
reasonable
rational
non-judgemental

Child: we all have a child in us, no matter how old we are!

What kind of behaviour does our child show?

loving	angry
curious	rebellious, manipulative
spontaneous	frightened
adventurous, playful	fights authority, protesting
trusting	sulky
creative	tantrummy
eager	attention seeking

Yes, we all copy all this behaviour too!

Reflect: **Can you recognize your PAC behaviour?**
What happens when you meet someone else's PAC?

This is where it gets interesting!

If you are coming from your adult state when you are with another person, you are likely to 'hook' the adult state in that person. However, if you are being like a bossy or critical parent, you are likely to 'hook' the sulky or tantrummy child in that person (no matter how old they actually are!) or vice versa. Does that make sense?

So positive adult-to-adult, parent-to-parent, and child-to-child interactions give us a feel-good feeling, whereas negative parent-to-child and child-to-parent interactions don't feel so good.

Reflect: **When someone is shouting at you, how does it make you feel?**
However, what state does that hook in you?

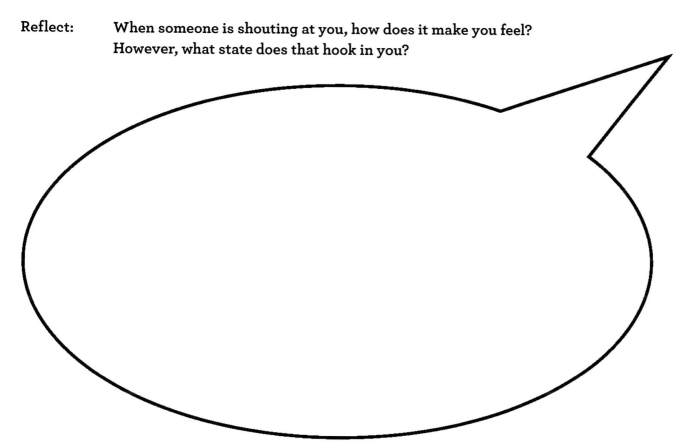

Do: What can you do to stay or step back into your 'adult' to stop an all-out war erupting! Then watch what happens between you as you can 'hook' their adult too and diffuse the situation. Try it!

NOTES

Change what you want to or need to change.

I can do this!

Keep going.

Having a go.

Preparing to change.

Maybe I need to change!

hat change!

Ooops!

Change: what do you want or need to change?

Change takes time, and it is important to know where you are in the stages of change.

Stages of Change

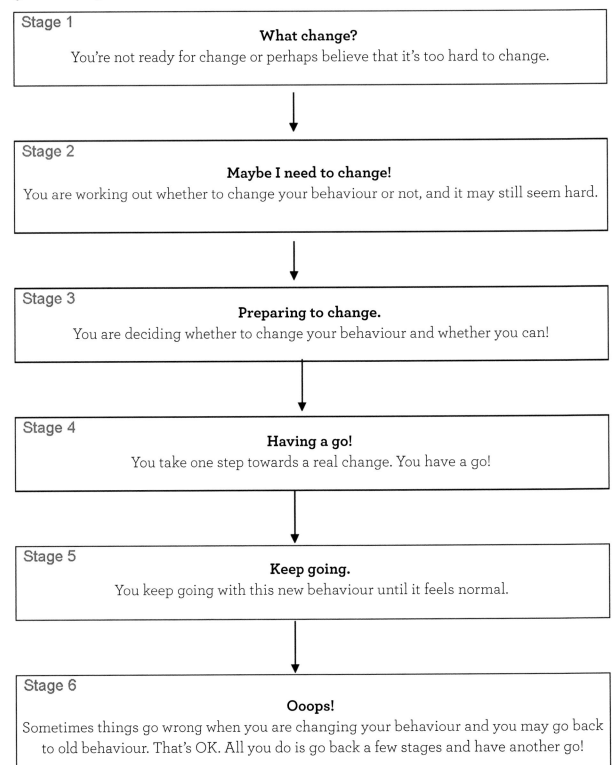

Stage 1

What change?

You're not ready for change or perhaps believe that it's too hard to change.

Stage 2

Maybe I need to change!

You are working out whether to change your behaviour or not, and it may still seem hard.

Stage 3

Preparing to change.

You are deciding whether to change your behaviour and whether you can!

Stage 4

Having a go!

You take one step towards a real change. You have a go!

Stage 5

Keep going.

You keep going with this new behaviour until it feels normal.

Stage 6

Ooops!

Sometimes things go wrong when you are changing your behaviour and you may go back to old behaviour. That's OK. All you do is go back a few stages and have another go!

Reflect: **What stage do you think you are in right now?**
What stage do you want/need to be in?

Do: **Use this exercise to help you.**

What do you think you want or need to change about yourself? What do others think?

Myself
_____

I want/need change
_____

Why?
_____

How would I feel if I made this change?
_____
_____

Parents/Carers
They want me to change

_____

Why?
_____

How would they feel if I made this change?
_____

How would I feel?
_____

Teachers

They want me to change
_____

Why?
_____

How would they feel if I made this change?
_____
_____

How would I feel?
_____

Good Friends

They want me to change
_____

Why?
_____

How would they feel if I made this change?
_____

How would I feel?
_____

Choose **SMART** goals.

Choose **SMART** goals.

How did you get on with the One-Minute Motivator? It is a very quick and useful way to help yourself in all sorts of situations.

Now let's look at setting and achieving goals in a bit more detail.

SMART stands for

Specific: When you are setting yourself a goal, it is really important that you are clear about what you really want to achieve.
Use the three Ps to help you.

State your goal using 'I.' That makes it *personal* to you.
Use *positive* words and as if it has already been achieved—*present* or now.
Your brain believes whatever you tell it! And the future doesn't exist; you only have now.

So instead of 'I don't want my name to go on the consequences board,' say,
'I can get on with my work in class.'

Measurable : How will you know that you are working towards your goal?

If we use the example above, you will know because you will not get to see your name on the consequences board!

Appealing: Your goal has got to appeal to you, or it just won't happen!

What's appealing about not seeing your name on the consequences board? That's pretty obvious, isn't it?

Realistic: How realistic is your goal? Be honest with yourself here without being negative.

If you hear a voice in your head that's saying, 'Don't be ridiculous. You can't do that!' remember to observe and let it go.

However, you also do not want to set yourself up to fail! Remember to remain non-judgemental with yourself. Then the goal you say should be *one step* towards 'I can get on with my work in class.'

For example, 'I can stop my name going on the consequences board tomorrow.'
This is where the last letter of SMART comes in.

Timed: By stating 'tomorrow,' you are setting a realistic deadline towards your goal.

Do: Now have a go. Choose a simple goal that you would like to achieve, and take it through SMART. Remember to use personal words and positive words.

Specific

Measurable

Appealing

Realistic

Timed

NOTES

Enjoy **GROW**ing with
your inner coach.

Options
What can you do to move one
step towards your goal?

If you knew you could do
anything, what would you do?

Reality: What support do you
want/need?

Reality: What have you
tried so far, if anything?
How did that go?

Reality: What's going
on right now?

Goal: What specifically
do you really want to
achieve?

**How will you
celebrate!**

Who can support you?
What do you want them to do?
What's the conversation you
need to have with them?
What will you say? When?

Way forward: What could
stop you? How will you get
over this?

:

Way forward: When are
you going to do it?

Way forward: What
are you actually
going to do?

Way forward: Which idea
excites you most?

NOTES

Energise your mind and body.

Energise your mind and body.

Living a healthy, fulfilling life is what it is all about.

How important is water? Did you know the following?

	water (%)
The human body	60%
Blood	92%
Brain	75%
Muscles	75%
Bones	22%

(www.waterinfo.org/resources/water-facts)

A human can survive for a month or more without eating food but only a few days without drinking water.

Reflect: **How much water do you drink every day?**

Water can also come from foods such as cucumber. However, keeping yourself hydrated with water/ fluid is essential.
If you find yourself getting tired or finding it hard to concentrate, it could be because you are dehydrated.
You need up to 1.2 litres of fluid per day. More if you are doing sport!

Do: **Keep yourself topped up with water by taking sips throughout the day.**

Reflect: How old is your body?

Did you know that your body is constantly renewing itself?

How long it takes depends on the different cells. Here are a few examples.

Cells	Renewal Time
Skin	10–30 days
Lungs	8 days
Lining of your gut	2–4 days
Skeleton	7–10 years

What does your body use to make new cells and replace old cells? Food.

Whatever you eat is what the body can use. The quality of food you put into your body directly affects the quality of the cells it can then make.

So the body you have now has been made from the food you ate last month, last year, etc.! Junk in equals junk cells! What a thought!

What kind of body do you want next year? When you are 30 years old? 60 years old?

Your body also likes and needs to move! What do you do each day to move it?

Again, this does not have to be an extreme sport!

Simply walking more is good. Not sitting for long periods is also important.
Break up the social media sessions with stretching and moving your legs.

Learn about Mindfulness
Stress can work on the brain and body both positively (helps you to do things!) and negatively (can make you anxious and worried).

Mindfulness helps you to live in the now. Mindfulness is about freeing yourself from regrets about the past and worries about the future.

Check out: 'The Mindful Teen' Dr. Dzung X Vo

Trusted adult
If you ever feel unsafe and want to talk to a trusted adult,
check out: **www.childhelplineinternational.org** for a contact in your country.

Reflect and Do: Keep a wellness diary for a week. Use a new page for each day.   Write everything down that passes your lips.   No cheating and no exceptions!

My 7 day wellness diary

	Day _____
Breakfast	
Lunch	
Dinner	
Snacks throughout the day	
Water/fluid Number of glasses	
Time spent on gadgets!	
Time spent in the fresh air. What exercise have you done?	

Do: Check out the Eatwell Guide. If you know that you need to make a few changes, then use the GROW model to help you to make those changes. Even small changes can have a big impact on how energized you feel.

Design your own life.

Design your own life. Don't leave it to chance or someone else.

By now I hope that you are happy working with your inner coach to make simple changes that can have a big impact on how happy you are with certain areas of your life.

So let's finish by looking at every aspect of your life so that you can continue to move forward confidently and in control of your future.

Do: **The Eight Fundamentals Exercise**

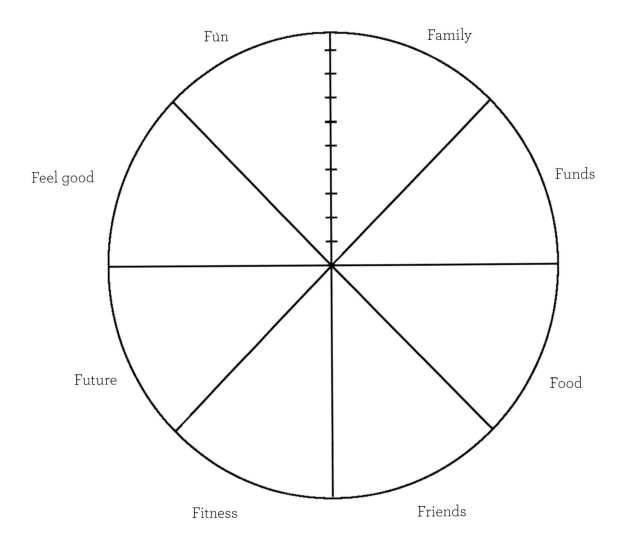

When the eight sections represented above are in balance, then life flows.

Regard the centre of the wheel as 0 and the outer edge as 10. Estimate how happy you are within each area of your life, with 0 being not very happy and 10 being very happy.

Draw a straight line between each section to create a new outer edge. The new perimeter of the circle represents your current position.

If this were a real wheel, how bumpy would the ride through your life be?

Below are some ideas to stimulate thinking!

Future

How happy do you feel with the way your future is shaping up?
How happy are you with

- your schoolwork?
- your personal development?
- your ambitions?
- your job prospects?

Funds

This section relates to your relationship with money.

- How happy are you with the way you manage money?
- How do you get money?
- How do you spend money?
- How do you manage your money? What do you need to learn here?

Family

- How happy are you with the relationship that you have with your family?
- What do you value about your family?
- What contribution do you make to your family?
- What would you like to change about your relationship with your family?

Friends

- How happy are you with the friends you have?
- How influenced by your friends are you?
- What would you like to change about your relationship with your friends?
- How many real friends do you have as opposed to Facebook 'friends'?

Fun

- How much fun do you have in your life?
- What do you do to have fun?
- What would you like to do to have fun?
- How much time do you spend out in the fresh air?

Food

- How happy are you with your relationship with food?
- What would you like to eat more of?
- What would you like to eat less of?

- What would you like to drink more of?
- What would you like to drink less of?

Fitness

- How happy are you with your level of fitness?
- How much exercise do you get each week?
- What do you do for exercise?
- What would you like to do for exercise?
- How much exercise would you like to do each week?

Feel Good

- How happy are you about the way you treat yourself?
- How much time do you spend on social media, and how does this make you feel?
- What things do you do each day that make you feel good about yourself?

Now select one section to start with that you would like to make a change in, and use the GROW model to guide you to work out what you plan to do.

Finally!

Keep looking at the world through the eyes of endless possibility.

Never doubt that you are capable of achieving anything that you put your mind to.

Continue to listen to the brilliance in you.

Never give up on yourself.

Have a great life!

Additional Resources

My Seven-Day Wellness Diary

	Day _____
Breakfast	
Lunch	
Dinner	
Snacks throughout the day	
Water/fluid	
Number of glasses	
Time spent on gadgets!	
Time spent in the fresh air.	
Exercise you have done	

The GROW Model

Goal	What specifically do you really want to achieve?
Reality	What's going on right now?
	What have you tried so far, if anything? How did that go?
	What support do you want?
Options	What can you do to move one step towards your goal? 1. 2. If you knew you could do anything, what would you do? 3. 4.

Way Forward	What idea excites you most?
	What are you actually going to do?
	When are you going to do it?
	What could stop you? How will you get over this?
	Who can support you? What do you want them to do?
	What's the conversation you need to have with them?
	What will you say and when?
	How will you celebrate?

The Eight Fundamentals

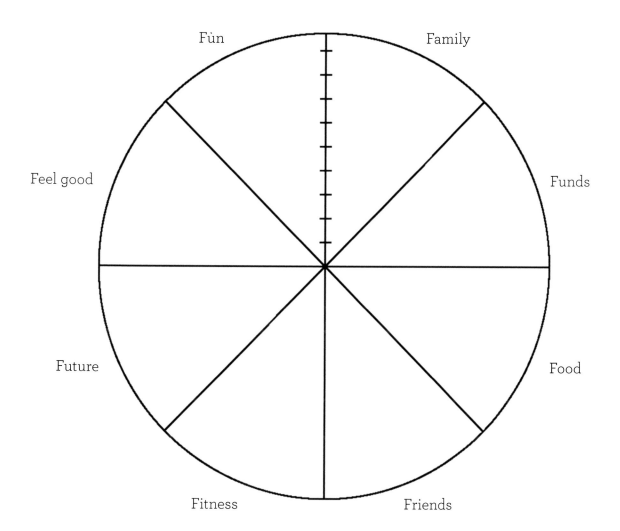

Printed in the United States
by Baker & Taylor Publisher Services